OCEAN ADVENTURES

THE PACIFIC OCEAN

Written by
Rebecca Phillips-Bartlett

KidHaven
PUBLISHING

Published in 2026 by
KidHaven Publishing, an Imprint of Greenhaven Publishing, LLC
2544 Clinton St., Buffalo, NY 14224

Written by: Rebecca Phillips-Bartlett
Edited by: Noah Leatherland
Designed by: Ker Ker Lee

Cataloging-in-Publication Data
Names: Phillips-Bartlett, Rebecca, 1999-.
Title: The Pacific Ocean / Rebecca Phillips-Bartlett.
Description: Buffalo, NY : KidHaven Publishing, 2026. | Series: Ocean adventures | Includes glossary and index.
Identifiers: ISBN 9781534552067 (pbk.) | ISBN 9781534552074 (library bound) | ISBN 9781534552081 (ebook)
Subjects: LCSH: Pacific Ocean--Juvenile literature. | Marine ecology--Pacific Ocean--Juvenile literature.
Classification: LCC GC771.P45 2026 | DDC 551.46'14--dc23

Printed in China

CPSIA compliance information: Batch #QW26KH: For further information contact Greenhaven Publishing LLC at 1-844-317-7404.

Please visit our website, www.greenhavenpublishing.com. For a free color catalog of all our high-quality books, call toll free 1-844-317-7404 or fax 1-844-317-7405.

Find us on

Photo Credits – Images courtesy of Shutterstock.com, unless otherwise stated.

Cover & Recurring – Romaine W, Nastya Vaulina, alazur. 2–3 – Frederick Millett. 4–5 – Kingppin, Lukas Gojda, BlueBackIMAGE. 6–7 – PorcupPaulo Figueiredo Junior, Aloia Photography. 8–9 – DOERS, OZGIOUN SAMPRI, Allen.G. 10–11 – phmarcosborsatto, Mike Workman. 12–13 – Maximillian cabinet, BEST-BACKGROUNDS. 14–15 – Mark A. McCaffrey, Podolnaya Elena, Tracey Jones Photography, Ethan Daniels. 16–17 – David A Litman, Kat ferrer, Circumnavigation. 18–19 – Kevin Le , Danita Delimont. 20–21 – Richard Whitcombe, Rich Carey. 22–23 – IVAN KUZKIN, Sergey Uryadnikov.

CONTENTS

WORDS THAT LOOK LIKE THIS CAN BE FOUND IN THE GLOSSARY ON PAGE 24.

OCEAN ADVENTURES

Grab your life jacket and climb aboard! We are going on an ocean adventure. Before we set sail, let's cover the basics. Oceans are very large pools of salt water. Earth has five main oceans.

Have you ever heard someone call Earth "the blue planet"? It has this name because almost three-quarters of Earth is covered by oceans. Oceans are home to many living things. They are very important places.

THE PACIFIC OCEAN

The Pacific Ocean is the world's largest and deepest ocean. It is larger than all the land on Earth. The Pacific Ocean is split into two parts—the North Pacific and the South Pacific.

THE PACIFIC OCEAN IS BETWEEN ASIA, AUSTRALIA, AND THE AMERICAS.

In 1520, an explorer called Ferdinand Magellan named the Pacific Ocean. The word "pacific" means "peaceful." Ferdinand Magellan thought the ocean looked very calm. Let's find out if he was right!

PLACES IN THE PACIFIC OCEAN

The Mariana Trench

The deepest part of the Pacific Ocean is called the Mariana Trench. The deepest part of the Mariana Trench is around 7 miles (11 km) deep. This is the deepest place on Earth!

LOTS OF ANIMALS IN THE MARIANA TRENCH MAKE THEIR OWN LIGHT. THIS IS CALLED BIOLUMINESCENCE.

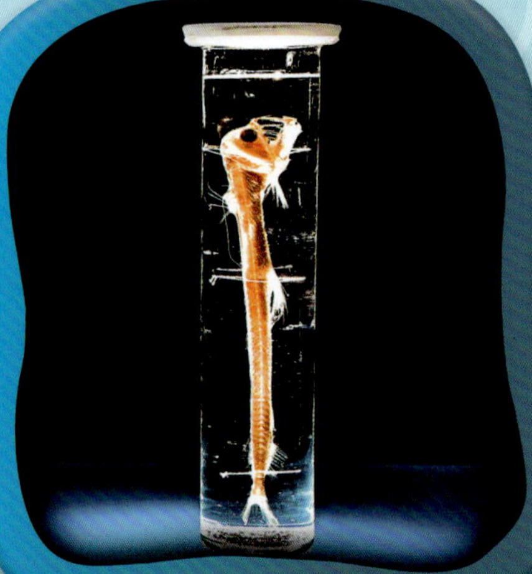

The Ring of Fire

The Pacific Ocean is surrounded by the Ring of Fire. The Ring of Fire is home to three-quarters of the world's active volcanoes. When volcanoes erupt, hot, melted rock called lava explodes out of them.

The Great Barrier Reef

The Pacific Ocean is home to the largest coral reef in the world, the Great Barrier Reef. Coral reefs are made of creatures called coral. They are home to thousands of other sea creatures.

THE GREAT BARRIER REEF IS NEAR AUSTRALIA.

Islands

Islands are pieces of land that are surrounded by water. The Pacific Ocean has around 25,000 islands. Fiji is a group of over 300 islands. The largest island in the Pacific Ocean is New Guinea.

WEATHER

Different parts of the Pacific Ocean can be very different temperatures. The temperature can also change throughout the year. Temperature changes cause wind. When wind travels over tropical water, it gets stronger and stronger.

Sometimes, this wind swirls around in a powerful storm. Storms that form over tropical oceans are called typhoons, cyclones, or hurricanes. Some of the strongest and most dangerous storms start in the Pacific Ocean.

FISH

Pink Salmon

Thousands of different fish live in the Pacific Ocean. Pink salmon live in the cold parts of the ocean. When they are ready to have young, salmon leave the ocean and travel to rivers.

In warm coral reefs, some fish are brightly colored. Others use camouflage to blend into the coral.

Reef Stonefish

Reef stonefish are mostly brown or gray with bumpy bodies. They are the most venomous fish on Earth.

CAN YOU SPOT THE STONEFISH?

MAMMALS

Sea Otters

Sea otters live near land in the North Pacific Ocean. They mostly eat clams and urchins. Like all mammals, otters need air to breathe. They float on their backs while they rest and eat.

Sometimes, otters wrap themselves in seaweed so they do not float away.

Whales

Many animals move from one place to another throughout the year. This is called migration. Lots of whales, such as humpbacks and blue whales, use the Pacific Ocean as a path for their migrations.

WHALES COME TO THE SURFACE TO BREATHE AIR THROUGH BLOWHOLES.

BIRDS

Bald Eagles

Many birds live near water and eat fish. Bald eagles mostly eat salmon and trout. They hunt by swooping down and grabbing fish out of the water with their feet.

SOMETIMES, BALD EAGLES STEAL FOOD FROM OTHER BIRDS RATHER THAN HUNTING FOR THEMSELVES.

Galápagos Penguins

The Galápagos Islands are a group of islands in the Pacific Ocean. These rocky islands are home to Galápagos penguins. Unlike most birds, penguins cannot fly. Instead, they are excellent swimmers.

OUR CHANGING OCEANS

Everything in the ocean is connected. If one thing changes, other things will be affected. For example, if we catch too many fish, other animals may not have enough food.

The Great Pacific Garbage Patch is a large patch of trash in the ocean. We can stop the Great Pacific Garbage Patch from growing by using less plastic and getting rid of our trash responsibly.

THE GREAT PACIFIC GARBAGE PATCH IS DANGEROUS FOR ANIMALS.

EXPLORING THE OCEAN

The Pacific Ocean is huge! From tropical typhoons to venomous stonefish, we have certainly seen a lot of this ocean. Do you think the Pacific Ocean is as peaceful as Ferdinand Magellan believed?

There is still lots of ocean left to explore. As we explore, we must be careful and kind to the living things that make their homes in the oceans.

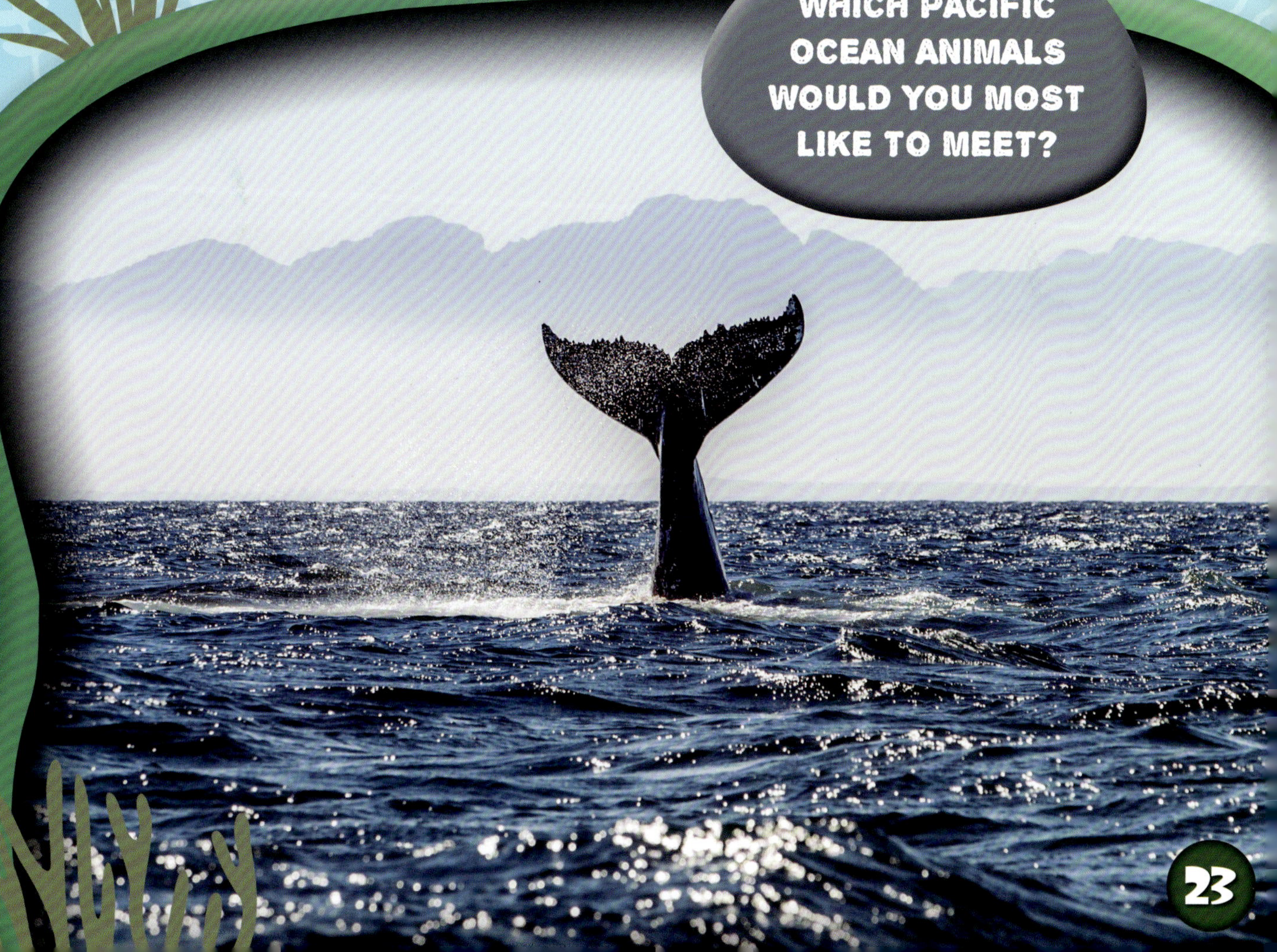

WHICH PACIFIC OCEAN ANIMALS WOULD YOU MOST LIKE TO MEET?

GLOSSARY

active volcanoes volcanoes that have erupted within around the last 12,000 years or could erupt again

camouflage a way of hiding by blending into the surroundings

mammals animals that are warm-blooded, have a backbone, and make milk to feed their young

quarters four equal parts of something

temperatures how hot or cold something is

tropical to do with very warm and wet areas

venomous able to inject a harmful substance called venom through a bite or a sting

INDEX